D1390716

Funny, Furry And Frightening - A Collection Of Poems For Children

Edited by Jessica Woodbridge

Poetry by the People
for the People

First published in Great Britain in 2005 by:
Anchor Books
Remus House
Coltsfoot Drive
Peterborough
PE2 9JX
Telephone: 01733 898102
Website: www.forwardpress.co.uk

© Copyright Contributors 2005

SB ISBN 1 84418 412 9

Foreword

Anchor Books is a small press, established in 1992, with the aim of promoting readable poetry to as wide an audience as possible.

We hope to establish an outlet for writers of poetry who may have struggled to see their work in print.

The poems presented here have been selected from many entries, and as always editing proved to be a difficult task.

I trust this selection will delight and please the authors and all those who enjoy reading poetry.

Jessica Woodbridge

Editor

Contents

The Poems

Childhood Fun

Running around the house
In and out of doors
Chasing each other
Leaving footprints on the floors

We're having great fun
Running around the house
I'm a tomcat
Brother is the mouse

Now brother is a cowboy
And I'm an Indian brave
He has to catch me quickly
His wagon train to save

I've made a stick spear
And his fingers are his gun
We don't need expensive toys
To have a load of fun

When all our games are over
All our playing done
It's up the wooden hill
Tired from all our fun.

Sean Sessions

The Shelter

Helter-skelter we ran to the shelter,
Sally McGinty and me.
We ran to the shelter helter-skelter,
Under the sycamore tree.

Crawling and cloistered we cuddled within.
Soothed by the sycamore's shade.
Tightly trembling together,
Glad of this gloomy glade.

'Did you see it?' said Sally.
'I think so,' said I.
'Was it big and black,
With a piercing cry?'

'It was brown, I think, and it loped along.
Its snout was sniffing the air,
It had two beady eyes and a furry coat,
Just like a big brown bear.'

'Are you certain?' said Sally.
'I think so,' said I, 'but I couldn't see for the trees.'
'We'll stay here a while till it passes,
To calm our knocking knees.'

'Let's leave this shelter and run helter-skelter.'
'Oh, Sally McGinty you're bold.'
Helter-skelter we ran from the shelter,
We didn't need twice to be told.

Dorothy Foster

A Pet Parrot

I once had a pet parrot
Called Joey
Who thought he could sing
Just like David Bowie
So he sang and he sang
Until his voice box
Went twang
Now all he sounds like
When he sings
Is an old black crow.

Donald John Tye

Last Night And The Night Before

Last night and the night before,
There was a loud bang upon my bedroom door.
I opened it to find, a strange scary sight,
My mother had a fright,
When I told her what I saw.

The old lady from number six,
Who lives with her black cat, whose name is, Twix,
Stood in front of me with her broomstick,
And told me to come quick,
For out on the landing her dragon was sick.

His usual red face was yellow and green,
The most peculiar sight I have ever seen!
He looked awfully tired and unusually lean.
I gave her my blanket to cover him quick,
For I didn't like to see the poor dragon sick.

I wonder if tonight will be the same as before,
The usual bang upon my door,
The pair outside on the landing floor.
The lady in her dressing gown,
And her dragon wearing his sad frown.

Katie Cheetham

Nursery Rhymes

Santa Claus had aching jaws
One snowy Christmas Eve
So he sent for his elves
Who did his work themselves
While Santa had some leave

Mary Jane was rather plain
With her pigtails and glasses
But she grew up quick
And became the pick
Of all the girls in the classes

Little Mary caught a fairy
At the bottom of the garden
She put it in a tin
But thought it was a sin
So released it as a pardon

Little Freddy lost his teddy
One afternoon at the zoo
He saw the giraffes
And started to laugh
For Teddy was spotted too

Young Billy felt a bit silly
One day while at school
He had two shoes right
But one was too tight
He really was a fool

There was once a ginger cat
Who thought he was a bat
For with a frown
He hung upside down
Then landed on the mat.

Terry Daley

Fruitful Harvest

Look all around
Plants and animals on the ground
Look at you
Look at me
The green and red holly
Look, look to the sky
Smell the cranberry pie
Tell me, can you see my eye?
A picnic and I-Spy
Beginning with 'G', no letter 'I'
Hooray, a portrait of Guy Fawkes
Or a gentleman
In an ice cream van
How many stars in starshine?
All I know is Mr Sheen
But the better the devil you know
Than the devil you don't
Hmm . . . puddings earthlings
Time to get some proper wings
And so it was to fly
With stuffed feathers
And my eagle eyes.

Hardeep Singh-Leader

Little Mouse

Little mouse, where are you going
In such a great hurry today?
Winter is fast upon your tail
So hurry, don't lose your way.

I watched her run along a leafy trail
As the autumn wind blew so chilly,
Between the tree roots her tail disappeared
As I thought to myself, *how silly!*

I imagined her entering a cosy room, there
All cheery with firelight glowing,
Children and Grandma ready to welcome
As winter mitts, they sat about sewing.

Over the fire, a bubbling pot of stew
All ready and warming for supper,
But, not before Mrs Mouse relaxed
With her steaming, honeyed cuppa.

The table set, for all that were present
Tiny napkins next to each spoon,
Little ones impatiently waiting
Hoping supper would be served very soon.

And so by firelight, they quickly ate
All cosy beneath their oak tree,
The autumn wind gathered its strength
Almost taking my feet from under me.

It was late that night, as I fell asleep
When a vision popped into my head,
Of tiny heads with night caps on
All tucked up, toasty warm in their bed.

Sue Meredith

The Night Of The Witches

Tonight's the night
When the witches fly
By the light of the moon
Way up in the sky

They fly on their broomsticks
Around and around
Swishing and swooping
Till they touch the ground

Look at their shadows
Can you see
And what's that glowing
Through the trees?

Now don't be scared
It's only the moon
Lighting the way
For witches on brooms

Down they all come
Casting their spells
It's Hallowe'en night
And all is well.

Patricia Lay

The Kaffoon That Kaddanced In The Dark

With his baldy belly and his feet so smelly,
The kaffoon is the daftiest dog there ever did was.
Oh the kaffoon - the kaffoon that kaddances in the dark.

He sleeps all day and he sleeps all night,
Just getting him out of bed takes us all our might.
That's the kaffoon - the kaffoon that kaddances in the dark.

With his big wet nose and long pointy toes,
In-between sleeps he likes nothing better than to doze.
Wake up kaffoon - the kaffoon that snoozes in the dark.

His idea of exercise is a five minute stroll in the park,
When he kaddashes around in circles, chasing his tail for a lark.
That's you lazy boy - the kaffoon that kaddances in the dark.

When his tea's on the table, he stretches and yawns,
In case he just might be able, to work up an appetite.
Get up now fatty - the kaffoon that kaddances in the dark.

Kaffoon, kaffool, kaffooey or kaffoodle,
We don't know your breed but you sure ain't no poodle.
You're our kaffoon - the kaffoon that kaddances in the dark.

Charles Christian

Flu

You have pains in your arms
And pains in your head
And pains in your back
And you feel half dead.
Your nose is blocked
You just keep sneezing
Your chest is tight
Forever wheezing.
You feel so tired
That you want to sleep.
You ache so much
That you want to weep.
You feel so cold
That you stay in bed.
Your face is white
But your nose is red.
You stay at home
For quite a short term.
Then back to school
To spread the germ.

Robert Peirce

Gnome Gnonsense

Gned the gnome lived in a gnut
But that was before he retired
And his magic became uninspired
And his spells lost their sparkle
And his wand went limp - limp - limp
And hopped away as a frog.

Archgnome looked down
With a frown
On Gned.
'Time to be dead Gned,'
He said.

A-painting the leaves in autumn
A-popping the buds in spring
A-polishing up the raindrops
A-making the harebells ring.

Dancing on top of the toadstools
With red paint on your toes
Cutting the shapes of the petals
To make a beautiful rose.

Oh! Tra-la-la, tra-la-lee
Welcome to Clacton-on-Sea.

High in a chestnut tree sits Gned
Painting the leaves bright red
Brown and ochre, tan and yellow
Happy fellow.

He's making pictures on every leaf
Good grief!
Landscapes, seascapes, well-designed
All signed
Gned.

(Clacton-on-Sea is where the home for retired gentlegnomes is situated.
This is not generally gnown)

Juliet Borland

Hidden Fear

Whisper in the night.
Scritch scratch in your ear.
Hidden under covers.
Bound by your fear.

A chill touches you.
Makes you want to scream.
Wrapped up in your covers.
Lost in a dream.

Cold sweat, can't move.
Dry breathing, close by.
Pull the covers tighter.
You don't want to die.

Ben Briggs

The Staffordshire Jug

Today was different as I knew it would be,
As I looked at my blue and white jug.
For I was transported into a new world
Up steep steps which led to pagodas.
I sat by a lake where above my head,
Two love birds now fluttered ecstatic
And on the water a sampan was paddled.
There were quaint little houses with white painted doors,
And a curved blue-white bridge where three coolies stood.
Trees bowed down with blooms,
Fragrant frangipan scented.
Bemused now, my senses slowly surfaced
And I knew then my fantasy no longer existed.

Biddy Redgrove

My Favourite Weather

I love it on a winter's day
When the wind is blowing,
I love to run outside and play
Especially when it's snowing.

I love to be out in a storm
Walking down the lane,
Mummy wraps me up quite warm
Against the wind and rain.

I love to go out in a gale
When the wind is high,
And see my kite fly up and sail
Right across the sky.

I love to see the snowflakes fall
When all the world looks white,
And all my playmates come to call
Me for a snowball fight.

But most of all I love it when
The fog is thick and deep,
And darkness starts to fall and then
Into my bed I creep.

Denise Castellani

Saucy Dorsey

Saucy Dorsey wiped her chin,
And stuck another finger in,
Looking at the dripping blob,
She opened wide her drooling gob,
And swallowed all the gunk inside,
The evidence she'd need to hide!

Saucy Dorsey grabbed the towel,
And mopped her finger with a scowl,
She'd left a mark for all to see,
They'd know she'd touched,
The special tea.

Saucy Dorsey had a plan,
She knew it was a cunning scam,
She'd hide the towel,
That's what she'd do,
And then she'd blame it,
All on you!

M Wilcox

Teddy

Teddy bears wait in a window, like soldiers waiting for a dance.
Dressed in waistcoats of finery, frills, bows and hats.
A little boy passed the window one day
                         his nose up against the glass.
His mother tugged on his arm, his interest had not passed.
'Ooh teddies, I love teddies, I want them all!
Teddies in my bedroom, teddies big and small!'
Timmy's mum could not disappoint her child.
'Oh alright, we will go inside, but only for a little while.'
Oscar the teddy bear spied the little boy with delight.
'Another child determined for a friend, perhaps it's my turn tonight!'
Timmy cast his eyes around the shelves,
He was searching for a particular friend.
There were so many to choose from, and so little time to spend.
'How about this one, a lovely red waistcoat and bow tie?'
But Timmy had seen the one he wanted, with his beady eye.
He wore a monocle, and looked distinguished,
                         sat there all by himself.
Oscar sat there delighted that he had been chosen,
                         it was lonely on this shelf.
'Oh Mummy! How about this one! The one with a lovely blue coat?
I could take him to the boating lake, he could be captain of my boat!'
The shopkeeper, an elderly man,
Had waited patiently to sell the bear.
He had made every teddy bear in the shop, made them all with care.
He gently laid Oscar on the counter,
And wrapped him up in tissue paper and a paper sack.
But just before he covered Oscar's face,
He winked, and Oscar winked back!
They were parting, after many years, the shopkeeper was sad.
Timmy was taking Oscar to a new home,
And for his old friend he was glad.
'Now Timmy you can't have Teddy until Christmas Day,
So you have some time to think of a new name, what do you say?'
'I think I will call him Oscar, no I think I will call him Ben.'
'But I think Oscar sounds very nice.'
'Okay I will call him Oscar then!'

Emma Lockyer

A Honeybee's Summer

Buzzing around from flower to flower,
The bumblebee braves that tiny shower.
Straight are those flights for nectar so mellow
Wherein it crawls with coat of yellow.
Many bright petals will open wide
Along the sunshine's golden glide.
Laden with dustings of pollen scattered,
Its heavy load seldom mattered.
Six miles of travel throughout that day,
Then back to its hive with full bouquet.
More bees are met as they hasten home
Each to enrich their honeycomb.
Constant there is that quest and joy
When teacakes are eaten by girl and boy.
The honeybag is kept by the bee
Where sometimes is found, its nose in a tree.
But there inside a resin pitches
And amber becomes a poor man's riches.

Arthur S Ford

Untitled

*(I wrote this poem in infant school when I was 7 or younger.
'Motor cars' is what we called cars in 1926!)*

If the rain was made of silver
Wouldn't we have fun
Gathering up the raindrops
Glittering in the sun;
Then we would be very rich
Like people up in town,
And I'd buy a motor car,
Go riding up and down.

Dorothy M Parker

Building Wishes

Build me a house right up to the sky
A hundred rooms wide and a thousand rooms high

Dig me a garden with flowers and trees
With a pond I can paddle in, up to my knees

Build me a house a thousand rooms high
So I can stand on the roof and touch the sky

I'll look down on the garden; I'll see the birds play
And when I get tired, I'll just . . .

fly away.

Suzan Round

Fizzy Feet

I'm known as 'Little Widdle',
or else as Heather Jane.
I'm not exactly normal.
It's tricky to explain.

My dad is tall and noisy.
My mum is short and sweet.
My sister's got teenitis,
but I've got fizzy feet.

They fizzle when it's bedtime.
They fizzle through the night.
They sizzle in the bedclothes
until the morning light.

Can't weigh them down with concrete.
Can't stick them down with glue.
My feet are just so fizzy!
Whatever can I do?

Jeff Vinter

There's A Monster In My Bedroom

Peeping from underneath the bedclothes,
There's a shadow across the room
If I open my eyes just a tiny bit I can make a shape out of the gloom
There's a monster in the wardrobe, he's here every single night
I don't want you to think I'm cowardly, but he gives me such a fright
I try very hard not to move so he doesn't know that I'm awake
I'm sure he hears my heart thumping, I'm sure he sees me shake
He doesn't really move about much and he doesn't make a sound
But it doesn't make a difference 'cause I know he's around
Mum says there's no such monster but I know that it's not true
I see him lurking in my bedroom, I do, I really do
I can hear his breathing from where I hide beneath the pillow
For his breath to be so loud he must be a really huge fellow
One day when I'm much bigger I'll ask him why he's there
Perhaps if I come jumping out I'll give him such a scare.

Now I can hear footsteps coming towards me through the night
Friends or foe I cannot tell until finally on goes the light
I carefully look across the room, the shadow is only mine!
I can go to sleep now; everything is going to be just fine.

Zenda Madge

The Brown Hen

We had a brown feathery hen named Dot,
She laid lovely brown eggs, quite a lot,
A nice brown egg, for breakfast each day,
The very finest a hen could lay.

Saw her pecking on the ground,
Went to see what she had found,
She was eating a wriggly, squiggly worm.
Dot's brown eggs, in future made me squirm.

Now when having an egg to dip my bread,
I'll have a nice white one for breakfast time instead.

Olive Young

Granddaughter To Gran

As I sat against the fountain with my finger up my nose
My thoughts go off a-wondering, could she really touch her toes?
And did she need to prove it, and did I really care
And was she only joking when she fell and bent her hair?
The ambulance came humming from the town upon the hill
As I wondered did she really need that stretcher and the crew?
She had only bent a little when her head began to sway
And over she did wobble with her legs all astray,
The funny thing to hit me was the way she touched her toes
She really didn't need to go and touch them with her nose.

The moral of this story is when you become a nan,
Never do the things you can't always, do the things you can . . .

Jackie Venables

Spoilt Child

I can get what I want if I stamp my feet,
If I make enough noise, I get what I want to eat,
Exactly what I want, very colourful, very sweet.

Mother gets so embarrassed when I jump up and down,
When the people on the next table raise their eyebrows and frown,
So I do my best to be really unpleasant, and behave like a clown.

Where did I learn this behaviour? To be so crude and coarse,
To jump up and down, to whine like a horse,
Where did I learn this childish discourse?
Why from my children of course!

Alan Bruce Thompson

Imagination

We only had a radio, no TV or a phone
No DVDs to sit and watch in silence on your own
No skateboards fast or rollerblades . . . computers or hard drive
Imagination! Yes that's all, as children played inside.

To think that I could close my eyes and be just anywhere
A cowboy chasing Indians or spaceman in the air
A pilot with his aeroplane or pirate in disguise
Imagination was the best inside these now closed eyes!

To see the seven wonders grand and never leave my chair
Or sail the seven seas again, the wind set mild to fair
A soldier for her majesty or guardsman on parade
These are the things that I became . . . imagination made.

I won a race at Silverstone, at Monte Carlo too
And rode the winning horse again at Aintree right past you
The winning goal at Wembley and the World Cup in Brazil
At 8 years old so famous now, imagine if you will.

You don't need wires or batteries or cell phones with a screen
Designer clothes or jogging shoes to be where I have been
I wish that children of today could see the things I saw
With eyes closed tight my fantasy and play there evermore.

Robert Eric Weedall

Red, The Squirrel

The squirrel awoke from his peaceful sleep
Safe and sound in the hole of a willow;
A conifer leaf he'd brought for a sheet
And some soft moss he used for a pillow.

He yawned and got up from his cosy bed
Now his stomach was hungry and hollow;
It groaned and grumbled and asked to be fed
And his throat wanted acorns to swallow.

He scurried outside, his fur shining red
For it blushed in the sun's warm embrace;
He crept along branches and checked overhead
Because hawks like the way squirrels taste.

No birds could be seen, he skipped to the ground
Where grass tickled pine cones on the floor;
He munched and chomped on this treat he had found
'Til it looked like a chewed apple core.

What should our furry friend have for dessert?
Maybe hazelnuts, berries or flowers;
But naughty grey squirrel had eaten them first
So his next meal might not be for hours.

But Red was clever, he'd hidden some nuts
In a top-secret place in the wood;
He clawed at the soil, began to dig up
Some delicious and wonderful food.

Then he ran home, (full - that is certain!)
With his bright, bushy tail in the air;
Drew the white web he used as a curtain
And relaxed in his orange-peel chair.

Deborah Headspeath

Two Little Doggies

Two little doggies awoke from sleep
Said, 'Now for a frolic, now for a leap,
Wake our master, go to the hall,
See if the leads are hung on the wall.
It's breakfast time, what shall we do?
The master is late and in a stew,
Worried and fretful we must change his mind,
Wag our tails and give him a sign
That we want to go to the fields,
Chase the rabbits to the wood,
A nice run and walk will do us all good.
Our master loves us, gives us praise,
We will do what he tells us, learn from his ways.'
Two little doggies, one fat, one tall,
'We'll help one another to get the leads from the wall.'

George Camp

Tinker Belle

I have a little friend
Her name is Tinker Belle,
She comes to see me every day
So now I know her well.

She sits on my doorstep
And calls to make me hear
Then dashes in through opened door
As soon as I appear.

When I'm in the garden,
She comes to watch the work
And follows me around out there
Makes sure I do not shirk.

Tinker Belle is pretty
As pretty as the flowers,
She plays with all the butterflies
But does not like the showers.

She once was run over
By a reversing car,
She took some time to recover
Afraid to go out far.

Now she visits neighbours
And purrs whene'er we meet,
Tinker Belle is a friendly cat
That lives across the street.

N M Beddoes

Hands Together

As I kneel down by my little bed,
Hands together, prayers to be said,
'I love my mum, I love my dad,
But my little brother drives me mad.
I wish he would go away,
If he shares his sweets he can stay.
Lord I really love him too,
But that's between me and you.'

Robin Morgan

Uncle George

My uncle George is a spry old lad
He's near on 93
There's no other treat he looks forward to
Than taking a lady out for tea.

He washes and combs his snow-white hair
And arranges it carefully
Three strands across and three strands back
And he's ready to go out for tea.

He polishes his gnashers as well as his shoes
In his socks no holes you'll see
His shirt is tidy, all the buttons done up
When he takes his lady out for tea.

He drives a little old vehicle
The covers turned back smartly
His lady friend likes to wave to her friends
When she goes out for tea.

Old George he had a favourite spot
And they sit side by side neatly
They like to overlook the lake
Whilst partaking of their tea.

Old George's car is a pushchair bold
And his lady friend two years old, you see
She really enjoys going out with Grandad
To drink a cup of tea.

Diana Blench

Childhood Memories Of A Poppy Field

A red expanse
    Of lace-like
Shimmering wings
    Red
    Against
Floating puff balls
    Meandering through
A 'forget-me-not' sky.
Interspersed
With stout white daisies
With marigold centres
    Inviting
Buzzy bees
    And flippery butterflies . . .

    Heaven in a childhood dream.

Hannah Yates

The Upside Downside Bird

Oh how I laughed when I first heard
about the upside downside bird.
Apparently, I've heard it said
its feet are where once sat its head.
And one wing flies the wrong way round
so consequently it has found
that it returns before it's gone,
which means that later whereupon
and contrary to what they say,
tomorrow is not another day.

Patrick O'Neill

Why Is Poo Brown? (Something You've Always Wanted To Know But Never Liked To Ask!)

So many things to learn about when you are only four!
Why can't we breathe in water?
What makes my daddy snore?
One thing I really want to know, but it makes my mummy frown
Is when I do a number two, why is it always brown?
I eat and drink a lot of things,
Like cornflakes, jelly, bread,
Orange juice and bananas,
And apples - green and red.
I really like baked beans on toast (they taste good going down)
But the poo is never orange
It's always boring brown!
So many different colours are there inside my food
There's a rainbow in my tummy and it really tastes quite good.
I know my body keeps the food it needs
And the rest goes down the loo,
But no matter what I never see
A rainbow in my poo!
I think I know the answer but I'm not sure if I'm right
the colours stay inside me and paint my dreams at night.
I dream of orange pufflebugs with fluffy yellow tails
They have green eyes, red noses
And they're very slow - like snails.
They let me climb upon their back and take me for a ride
Through a land that's full of colour (that all comes from my inside).
So when it comes to morning all that's left inside of me
To make my poo a colour
Is just plain brown, you see!

Deborah Anderson

Bertsplog

Bertsplog is a monster
Big, hairy and green,
But he's not very scary
And he's not very mean.

A soft, gentle creature
He was lonely and scared,
No friends of his own
Approach? No one dared.

A monster, an ogre,
A gruesome great thug,
But Bertsplog wasn't like that,
He only wanted a hug.

He lives in a forest
In a cave by a stream,
Where he once met a frog
Small, slimy and green.

'I'm sad,' said the frog
(Whose name was Grenville).
'Really?' exclaimed Bertsplog,
'That's just how I feel!'

And so they became friends
And hung out more and more,
Bertsplog learnt to catch flies
And Grenville learnt to roar!

Now neither are lonely
And alone are not seen,
A pair of best friends
A pair happy and green!

Tracy Caller

It's Not Fair

It's not fair
It's not fair
When they kick me and pull my hair
While others just stop and stare,
Every time that I go out
They get together and start to shout,
Sometimes I'm so scared to go to the shop
How far will they go before they stop?
I only want to be their friend,
When will this heartache ever end?

Diane Harbottle

Fantasy Land

On a magic carpet my friends and I
Went on a ride, into the bright blue sky.
We floated along in a gentle breeze
Over the valleys, the hills and the trees
To Fantasy Land where the fairies play
It never goes dark, the sun shines all day.
No ordinary people live there,
No witches or giants, nothing to scare.
There were some pink mice, of fondant made,
The fountain sparkled with fizzy lemonade.
We saw a chocolate cat on angelica grass,
It winked its eye as we walked past.
We could take our pick from the lollipop trees
Any flavour, whichever we pleased.
In Peppermint Castle on Daisy Hill
The king of the fairies lives there still.
Instead of snow it is vanilla ice,
In Fantasy Land it is really nice.
Who did we meet on our way back?
It was Father Christmas with an empty sack.
He gave a cheery wave, the reindeer said, 'Neigh.'
We were home again for Christmas Day.

Bridie Sutton

Crayon Box

Red sunrise,
Violet lotus,
Green pond,
White clouds,
Blue sky.

Yellow banana,
Purple aubergine,
Orange mango,
White milk,
Green grape.

Gold hair,
Black eyes,
Brown skin,
Pink nails,
Red lips.

I wish I had God's crayon box!

Smitha Bhat

One Foggy Night

Under the gentle orange street light,
hazy in the dark and foggy night,
I saw something small, ahead in the road,
lying quite still and all alone.

My heart began to pound with dread -
was it badly injured, or possibly dead?
What sort of animal could it be?
Should I try to help, or leave it in peace?

I crept a bit closer, I just had to know,
and then I saw its glistening bones;
long and bent and very thin -
like a spider wearing silver leggings.

Closer still, and I knew that this heap
left behind with no thought for its keep,
was definitely not a trodden-on jelly,
but a lonely little broken umbrelly!

Catherine Jeffrey

The Little Red Ant And The Bee

The little red ant climbed a tree
And came across a honeybee.
'What are you?' cried the ant in awe,
For he'd only been born the day before.
'I'm a bee,' said the stranger,
'And I help to make honey,
Flying around when the weather's sunny.'
'Oh,' said the ant, 'I wish I could too,
For I'd love to fly just like you do.'
Said the bee, 'It's hard work visiting flowers,
I really have to fly for hours.'
'Sounds to me,' cried the ant,
'Just like child's play
'Cause an ant walks a hundred miles a day.'
Then with a shrug he walked away.
I wonder what he's walking for?
His poor little feet must be so sore,
Thought the puzzled honeybee,
As he flew back to his hive for tea.

C Burnell

The Brighton Line 2002

Platform 13 - waiting
checking railways times
on the whistle blowing lines
including Clapham Junction

' . . . has changed - Brighton'
speaker message states
as hearing takes the strain
of whistle blows
on someone else's train
all other platforms duplicating.

'Change (something, something) Croydon,'
our announcer tries again
in separating chain
of jigsaw pieces in-between
other platforms' share of competition.

Hurried into carriages
by whistles' agitation.
Triple blast to driving cab
at southern end of platform.

Unmoving is the train
intended for East Croydon.
Perhaps the drive is indifferent
and is wearing ear protection.

Reg Baggs

Bedtime

How often have you heard it said,
'Come on my dear, it's time for bed.'
When all you really want to do
Is play another game or two.

Well, there's a way to do it all!
When you hear Mummy make that call -
Quite meekly off to bed you go
Don't even think of saying, 'No.'

When you are bathed and tucked up tight
And Mummy says, 'Put out the light,'
Give her a kiss, do as you're told,
She'll think you are as good as gold.

Then, when she's gone, the coast is clear
For you to play again my dear,
But *do* be wise, don't make a sound
Or Mum *will* hear you, I'll be bound.

The really clever thing to do
When sleepiness creeps up on you
Is - quickly tidy all your toys,
Remembering not to make a noise.

When Mummy comes to check once more
That all is well - just as before,
She'll never know you played a game
If everything still looks the same.

A R Carter

Far

When I look far out to sea,
I wonder where 'far' can be.
How far is 'far' I want to know
And if it's a place I'd want to go.
Would I be happy when I got to 'far'?
Is it a place where monsters are?
Would it be cold, would there be food
And would TV programmes be good?
The people there could be quite tall,
Or the size of mice, which is very small.
The dogs and cats could be bright blue
And have four tails and feathers too.
There might be rain and even snow.
I don't think 'far's' where I want to go!

Jenny J S Campbell

Mr Nobody, Horace And Me

I used to be scared of the dark,
And the things that go bump in the night,
But a magical thing happened last week,
And now I know in the dark, I'm alright.

It started with a tapping noise
That came from underneath my bed,
I could not move, I could not scream,
And then somebody said,

'I am Mr Nobody,
I'll help you with your fears,
Horace here's a spider,
he's been my friend for years.'

I slowly pulled the duvet back,
And saw it to be true,
A tall man with an orange face
And a spider of bright blue!

'Whenever you are scared,' said Horace,
'And you need a friendly face,
Just call our names and we'll appear,
To make the dark a nicer place.'

We sat up all night talking,
And as the hours went by,
The dark no longer scared me,
As the moon lit up the sky.

So now when it's dark in my bedroom,
My friends have helped me to see,
I'm no longer alone on a night-time,
There's Mr Nobody, Horace and me.

Danielle Madeley

No Tech Nana

Nana went all modern, got rid of her twin-tub,
Bought a brand new washer, my clothes to wash and scrub.
Had time to clean the house up, from the ceiling to the floor,
Then to my amazement, I couldn't open up the door!

Grandad bought a mobile, now I'm in a fix,
When I try to work it, my brain it fairly sticks.
The day he brought it home, he hadn't got a clue,
He had to get our ten-year-old to tell him what to do.
Her little fingers moved so fast, it set us in a spin,
Seems to me we old folks simply cannot win!

By the way, don't mention texts, or a DVD.
I'm afraid it's simply double Dutch to me.

Yet I'm really not quite useless, as you will shortly see,
When they want a fancy dress, who do they shout? Yes me.
I can make a Christmas dinner, I can cook a Yorkshire pud,
The biscuit tin I keep in they say is not half good.

High tech, low tech, call it what you like -
Sorry kids, but Nana's brain has gone on old-age strike.

Shirley Straw

Childhood

Once upon a golden time
So long ago on Cornish sands
Exploring with our fishing nets
Silent pools amongst the rocks.

We travelled down by hissing steam
Like Hogwarts' train- so very fast
Pulling coaches - cream and brown
Excitement when we saw the sea.

Oh happiness - those bedtime treats
Of stories, songs before we slept
Such lovely hours of carefree days
Clutching battered teddy bears.

We laughed and cried - with Mummy there
To wipe away our trickling tears
Her soothing words to make us smile
Safe within her gentle arms.

I am now a man of many years
Who sometimes wants to be a child
So young at heart - content with life
Playing with his model cars!

Steve Glason

Children's Prayer

Let the teacher of our class
Set us tests that we all pass.
Let them never ever care
About the uniform we wear.

Let them all clearly state
It's OK if your homework's late.
Let them say it doesn't matter
When we want to talk and chatter.

Let our teachers shrug and grin
When we make an awful din.
Let them tell us every day
There are no lessons, go out to play.

Let them tell our mums and dads
We're always good and never bad.
Let them write in their report
We are the best class they have ever taught.

D Sheasby

Nursery Tale

Sleeping Beauty fell asleep,
Little Bo-Peep lost her sheep,
Humpty Dumpty had a great fall,
Cinderella went to the ball.

London Bridge is falling down,
Jack fell down and broke his crown,
Pussy Cat frightened a mouse under a chair,
Johnny's so long at the fair.

Mary, Mary's garden is in bloom,
The cow jumped over the moon,
The little dog broke out in laughter,
They all lived happily ever after.

J Cross

Amy's Friend . . . Teddy Bear

When I was soft, white and cuddly,
Amy laid me on her bed,
When I was soft, white and cuddly,
Amy gave me a pillow for my head.
She would brush my fur and talk to me
And her secrets we would share,
Amy loved me so very much
Because I was her friend, Teddy Bear.
Wherever Amy went, I went too,
On picnics, to the seaside and even to the zoo.
All through school and her teenage years
I never once left her side,
When Amy laughed I was happy
But when she was sad, she held me and cried.
Amy has grown up now and somehow I have too,
My once soft, white fur, has got a tinge of blue.
Amy made me some clothes, because my fur is so thin,
I don't go on many outings now, I lie on Amy's bed and stay in.
We still share our secrets,
I know my Amy cares,
I still get lots of cuddles,
Because I'm Amy's friend . . . Teddy Bear.

Mary Plumb

The Haunted Wood

Step into the wood and listen,
Hear the noises of the night.
Patters, creaks, whispers, squeaks.
Keep your eyes right straight ahead,
Bright eyes watch your every tread.
Nocturnal creatures out to play,
They all shun the light of day.
The hunters and the hunted meet,
It must be so, they all must eat.
Dawn heralds yet another day,
Other creatures wend their way.
Butterflies, birds and insects too,
Bees and wasps and beetles queue,
To take their place in daylight hours,
And all around, the forest towers.

Ivy Allpress

The Toy Box

A little one-legged soldier leant in the corner of the box
Talking to the worn face of a fluffy fox
The three-legged donkey stumbled to and fro
As the doll with the broken eye asked, 'Where do all the
                                          broken toys go?'
'I've no idea,' said the Action Man with one arm.
'Maybe they go to a special hospital, away from harm,'
Said the bear with the missing nose.
'Well,' said Barbie, 'I can't find my missing clothes.'
'They must be amongst these bits and bobs at the bottom of this box,
Among these old jigsaw pieces and discarded building blocks,'
Said the jack-in-the-box who has a broken spring
And the old Buzz Lightyear held together with string.
'Funny,' said the three-wheeled car,
'How those humans are.
When new, they play with us for ages and never put us down,
But when they are careless with us, drop and break us, they
                                          leave us on the ground!'
'I do remember,' said the Game Boy with the cracked screen,
'That grown-up humans pick the broken toys up and put them
                                          in a black bag, this I've seen,
But after that, I have no idea.'
'They never come back,' said Raggy Doll, 'that's what it
                                          would appear.'
'Seems some don't have any care for us toys, or appreciation!'
Said the clown with the big red nose and the missing carnation.

Terry J Powell

Watch Out For Harry Huntsman

A few years ago my family moved to Brisbane —
        That's Brisbane, Australia, also known as Oz.
I've decided I should share my story as I'm over it now and because

If you ever go there it's something you should know
To keep your eyes peeled everywhere - up high and down low.

There isn't really a need to make all this fuss
As they are not at all dangerous to any of us.

You might not believe me as they look very scary
But that's only because they're big and they're hairy.

When you hang the washing out check the pot of pegs
For something big and hairy with eight big hairy legs.

They're not necessarily fat, some can be thinner
But it all depends if they've managed to catch some dinner.

As they don't make a web you'll never know they're there.
So all you can do is remember to enter a room then stare.

Look all around the floor and then high up on the wall,
They can jump as well you know, up high, really tall.

But you don't live in Oz - so I'm telling you this - why?
Because if you ever visit, I don't want you to cry.

There is always one place you should most definitely look.
Please look in every little nook!

As the days in Oz can be sunny and filled with extreme heat
So they like to hide in the cool - and sit underneath the seat.

So if you find yourself over in Oz and visiting the loo
What is the most important thing you shouldn't forget to do?

When you know that you're suffering from the sun and heat
Please do this one thing and don't forget to lift the toilet seat!

As when you've had a good day filled with fun and sun
The last thing you need is a hairy leg to tickle your little bum!

Lara Wiseman

The Little People

There's a place among my flowers
where the little people go,
a place for when they're tired
from all their to and fro,
elves and fairies rest there
with faces all aglow,
exactly where's a secret
that only they can know.

But one day in the garden
when the sun's an orange glow,
you may glimpse the little folk
helping flowers grow,
you must be very quiet
and keep your voices low,
and one day you may see them,
you never ever know!

Susan Carr

At The Bottom Of My Garden

There's a castle at the bottom of my garden
It's got soldiers and a moat and a bridge
It has towers and a dragon and everything
Can you see it? Look there! Under the hedge!

A witch lives in my garden
But she's never scary to me
Her house is behind the shed
If you look hard enough, you will see.

I have a wishing well at the bottom of my garden
With special magical powers
It's there look, next to the pond
In the middle of those pretty flowers.

There are fairies and pixies in my garden
Their home is the old apple tree
You'll have to come and visit one day
And have tea with them and me.

I wish you'd try a little harder
To share this wonderful place
Are you sure you can't see all these things?
They're as plain as the nose on your face.

Grown-ups can be so hopeless
It must be because they're tall
I don't want to lose my special world
I think I'll just stay small.

Louise Wheeler

Splishy-Splashy Mermaid

Splishy-splashy mermaid,
Swimming carefree in the sea,
Searching for some oysters,
To take back home for your tea.

But then a toothy shark came by,
And it started chasing you,
So into a cave you swam and hid,
For the shark was hungry, too!

T D Green

Scruffy

I've got a dog called Scruffy
If you meet him you'll know why
His coat's all dull and scraggy
And he's got a wonky eye
He slobbers on the carpets
Has mud upon his paws
He races all around the house
And muckies all the floors
I put his dinner on his mat
Into his doggy dish
He eats it in a greedy rush
Mouth open like a fish
When he gets really smelly
He can't come in our house
He tiptoes through the dining room
As quiet as a mouse
He thinks my mum's not noticed
That he's inside nice and hot
But Mum can smell him anyway
And inside he is not.

Anne-Denise Ferris

Strange Creature?

There is a strange wee creature, lives in my shed,
Whose legs number five, and whose fur is red.
He also wears dungarees that seem a little too long,
And a ten-gallon cowboy hat he bought in Hong Kong.
He's also visited Bali, China and Wigan Pier,
Caravanned in Yorkshire and camped on Windermere.
Eats peaches on toast at least five times a day,
Drinks gallons of Irn-Bru to stop him gong grey.
Wears wellie boots in summer and in winter then wears none,
Reads books upon books, upon books, but only for fun.
Has he no acquaintance, but friends he has by the dozen,
Has no real relations except for one cousin.
Visits two days to the chapel, and then the mosque for three,
The other two days are quiet, he likes to keep them free.
For Atheism he also enjoys for browsing at his leisure,
Everything else he does partake is purely for his pleasure.
But don't be dismayed, upset, frightened or bigoted through,
Because beneath it all, he's exactly the same as me and you.

Brian Lamont

An Artichoke

In the land of the Brie and the dangerous blue
An artichoke rolled on his way to the coup
Equipped with a gun, hard-holstered and green
A handsome young low-down fighting machine
Bred for the victory, unquestionably bold
He'd knock out an army of pesticides cold
Peas to the left, carrots to the right
'Wait for it, son, just kill on sight.'
Ketchup cascading, red as pure blood
Spilt on the altar where a tangerine stood
The valleys were filled with the cries of the slain,
'Hors d'oeuvres', 'hors d'oeuvres!' over again
A faithful old sprout wore a marmalade crown
A martyr to serve the cordon-bleu crown
Spread out on the line, the table-top Somme
Ranks of thin celery, aubergines and pomme
Called to self-sacrifice for incredible greed
A banquet of lies in a bedrock of need.

John Alan Davies

I'll Be A Vet

When I grow up I'll be a vet
Helping other people's pets!
I love animals, don't you see?
So to be a vet is what I'll be.

Dogs are my favourites,
Whether short or tall,
And rabbits and kittens . . .
I just love them all!

Birds, I think, are quite all right,
But they can be noisy when it's light!
Caged birds are a different thing,
But it's nice to hear them talk and sing!

I'd like to help them when they're ill.
They would come first . . . before the bill!
Caring for animals is my habit
As I have dogs, cats and lop-eared rabbit.

I couldn't eat animals. Oh no, not me!
So a vegetarian is what I'll be!
To help someone else's pet
Is why I want to be a vet.

Amy Robertson (10)

The Hippopotamus Went On A Big Red Bus

The hippopotamus went on a big red bus.
He wanted to go on a train but just as it started to rain
He got stuck in the gate which made him too late
So he had to go on a bus, the big red bus.

He tried to go on a bike
But the hills were too much of a hike
He ran out of puff and found it too tough
So the hippopotamus went on a big red bus.

The next time he tried to fly
But he didn't get very high
They said he was too heavy and a surcharge they would levy
So he had to go on a bus, the hippopotamus.

The hippopotamus liked the big red bus
There was plenty of room, the fare was cheap
The driver was happy and the horn went beep
Now the hippopotamus always goes by bus, the big red bus.

Lynda Hill

The Heretic's Ballad, 1549

The warmth of the sun and blue from the sky
Peer into my cell's isolation.
In just a few hours while my relatives cry
I will go to my last destination.
To burn at the stake for a faith that I know
Is saving my soul from destruction.
King Edward the Sixth wants his coffers to grow,
He's causing the Pope much disruption.

He is but a child in his father's new church,
Far too young to handle the throne.
Just like a shadow in Henry's view lurches
To sever relations from Rome.

Once when the churches together were one,
King Henry was named 'The Defender
Of Faith' by the Pope, but he wanted a son
And divorce. Yet from Rome, no surrender.
Lust and confusion within recent years
Is causing us total disaster.
I pray by tomorrow I'll not show my fears
For then I will meet my true Master.

P M Burdock

A Furry Friend

Walking through a graveyard late one night,
I came across a most hideous sight,
Its clothes were all dirty, torn and tattered,
But to the thing it didn't seem to matter.

A white haze surrounded this thing,
Then all of a sudden it started to sing.
The head was held under its arm,
Looking more closely, it looked like my nan.

'Hello,' I said, 'shouldn't you be down there?'
She stood very still and just stared.
'Can you see me?' I said to her,
Then I noticed she was covered in fur.

A loud moaning came from behind me,
Too scared, I didn't really want to see.
Something slimy touched my shoulder,
Wish I was brave and a lot bolder.

Tried to move my legs but they did not budge,
Was she angry with me and held a grudge?
Frightened and looking to the sky I saw stars,
Then she handed me two chocolate bars.

She looked at me and gave a wink,
And handed me a can of orange drink,
Starting to laugh she dropped her head,
I did so wish I was home in bed.

Out popped her own from the fancy dress
Bet I looked a terrible mess,
It was my friends, they had played a joke,
Thank goodness it was just a hoax.

Ali Ashley

I See!

Dragons, dragons, what do you see?
I see you, you see me.
I see slime dripping from your chin,
You are green.
You have a long, purple, spotty, spiky tail
Sliding behind you.
You live in a cave.
You are flying round my head tens of times.
Back I go, do you know what I said?
'What an adventure!'

Freya Sansum (6)

The Little Cloud That Strayed

The little cloud wandered
Across the blue sky,
The sun looked and shouted,
And made the cloud cry.
'I'm so sorry,' he said,
'I'll speak to the wind.
Please blow me back,
I shouldn't have sinned.'

Down below was a farmer,
Just praying for rain.
The little cloud's tears
Pouring down they still came.
He couldn't believe what he saw up above,
'Thanks, little cloud, I send you my love.'

Little cloud felt so happy
As wind blew him home,
'I must be more careful
And not stay or roam!'

Ena Field

Poppy

I like being in Grandma's garden
There's pretty flowers to see
And there's a birdbath on the lawn
I can watch while having tea.
A sparrow and a starling
Playing duck and dive,
I don't know any other birds
Cos I am only five.

I like being in Grandma's garden
Cos Grandma says I'm safe
No one can get in or out
With that lock fixed on the gate.
She has a blue gazebo
To shade us from the sun,
So we can sit and read some books
Or play cards just for fun.

I like being in Grandma's garden
When the sun's gone down.
We water all the flowers
To stop them going brown.
I'm learning all the names quite well
I know the names of three,
There are pansies and petunias
And a poppy . . . just like me.
Poppy Barsby!

Elizabeth Stevens

The Quest

The king rode through the mighty land
Upon his faithful steed
In search of his fair young maiden
From a prison she'll be freed.

To rescue her from this place
Was not an easy task
He would have to fight a beast from hell
Then she'd be in his grasp.

He ventured towards a dreary fort
And opened the mighty doors
To where the beast concealed itself
And to battle, it did soar.

Fire and flames did all spew out
Amidst the flesh and scales
The king beneath its writhing mass
Of lashing, jagged tails.

Once he had fought and slain the beast
He journeyed down and down
Till at last he found the maiden
And to give his queen a crown.

To prove he's worthy to his queen
He grabbed his mighty sword
And chopped the beast's bold head off
With a powerful and howling roar.

When all the blood had oozed away
Into the drains of hell
The mighty king of Averland
Had a tale to tell.

Samuel Edwards

My Golden Pencil

My golden pencil, my golden pencil
Very long like a parcel
And blunt in the cradle
Coupled with the eraser I handle.

But when it was sharpened
And created many sculptures,
Smaller and smaller it became
Completely, with the small eraser.

Oh my mighty golden pencil!
How I wonder you write forever,
Texts, comics, cartoons and sculptures,
But you depreciate every day in size.

Don A Adegbite

The Old Man In The North

Way up in the north where the cold winds blow
   and the polar bears burrow in great banks of snow
Lives an old man with frost on his nose
   and holes in his boots where he wriggles his toes
His eyes sparkle blue in a face that's all crinkly
   his cheeks are bright red and his false teeth are whistley
He smiles but it's hidden in a beard long and white
   with bristles that tremble as he laughs with delight
At the wishes and dreams of the children he loves
   who sing songs and write letters that fly like white doves
Up chimneys and over rooftops that glitter and glisten
   wanting desperately to know if the old man will listen
And on one night each year they excitedly wait
   to hear bells and hooves and a noise in the grate
And snuggling into bed each child tires to keep
   still as he listens, trying hard not to sleep
With milk and mince pies and carrots left near
   for someone very special the message is clear
'We wish, we hope, we dream we might
   have a visit from the old man in the north tonight.'

Linda Howitt

Memories Of Childhood

When I was little we lived at my gran's house.
My bed was in a creaky old attic
Which rustled at night and grew spiky shadows.
I hid my head deep under the pillows.

It felt such a long way to call to Mother,
Downstairs drinking tea with Grandpa and Gran.
On light nights I listened to folk in the park,
The park keeper's bell ring as it grew dark.

I loved to hear people laughing and shouting,
And sometimes a motorbike screeching by.
Then the park gates would shut with a giant clang.
In the stillness no voice called, no bird sang.

And I longed and I longed to drop off to sleep,
But too many thoughts whirled round in my head.
So I rolled and tossed until darkness fell,
Then somehow sleep cradled me and all was well.

One day I found I had a baby brother.
In time he was put in the room off mine.
He would stand up and wail and scream in his cot,
But, lonely no more, I slept like a top.

Margaret Gregory

I'll See You In The Morning - Maybe

What things come in the night?
What things are afraid to face the light?
Nocturnal dwellers in my room
Who only appear within the gloom
I hear a whisper, or the floor squeak
And bravely from under my covers I peek
And peer into the ghastly shadows
I had a nightlight, but the one I had though
Burned out earlier today
I know that under my bed stays
Something so horrible, I can't look
Something worse than the worst thing from any comic book
From my closet, a noise I hear
Are those red eyes that creepily leer
Back at me?
I wish I could see
I can barely make out my hand in front of my face
Much less the creatures with me in my dark space
I only want one thing on this night
That tomorrow I get a new bulb for my nightlight.

Deborah L Robinson

The Enchanted Garden

The colour of tulips caught my eye,
Red and yellow. A perfect garden, I had to sigh,
For there amongst the flowers, little girls sat,
They wore red flowered skirts, and little red hats.

I thought they were fairies busy at play,
Madeline, Immy, Melanie, Ella, what a special day.
Hannah, Nichole, Lydia too, were twirling in dance,
Cool scenes they created, a magical stance.

Peeping from behind the flowers was a little mouse,
Do you know it was Joseph, he'd come from his house.
What a dear little mouse he appeared to be,
Twitching his whiskers, wondering if the girls could see?

A handsome young man, Alex by name, played soft sweet music
like Peter Pan.
Echoing through the garden, 'Love Me Do', a heart-warming,
lovely, affectionate plan.
'Was that a nightingale in the garden we heard?'
Scott charmed us all with his heavenly voice, which echoed like birds.

Everywhere looked beautiful, filled with love to share,
When Auntie Shirley read *Martha Mouse*, a story showing care.
A story which was written by Auntie Pauline's hand,
Tick-tock went the clock when Madeline made a distinguished stand.
Her voice as soft as honey, 'So Long, Goodbye' she chose,
Gently through the garden, bringing this magical scene to
a remarkable close.

'Well done children, you were wonderful.
We look forward to seeing you next year.'

Lorna Tippett

Where's The Soap?

Someone's stolen the toilet seat.
The seat, the wood and the hole.
Someone's stolen the toilet seat
And they took the toilet roll.

Someone's stolen the toilet lid
It was black and had a crack.
Someone's stolen the toilet lid,
How I wish they'd bring it back.

Someone's stolen the toilet brush,
The one we used to clean.
Someone's stolen the toilet brush,
Now the water's turning green.

Someone's stolen the toilet bowl.
Unscrewed it from the floor.
Someone's stolen the toilet bowl,
Now we have to go next door.

Chris O'Rafferty

Fighting

'I can't hit him back,
he's bigger than me.'
I can't run away,
he's faster than me.
He punched me in the arm
and pushed me away.
I'm not having a good day.

'He hit me, 'cause I called him
a big, smelly poo.
He even hit my sister too.'
'Why?'
'Because she threw some
worms in his hair.
But Mum, it's just not fair.

His mummy took him in
and said he couldn't play.
But he said he'd come out
and get me another day.
My sister says
she'll punch his nose,
but I'll come off worse, again
I suppose.'

Kevin Kennie

Thomas And The Rabbits

I sat last night watching the rabbits hop
jumping about, flip, flap, flop
noses twitching, running around
sssh, be quiet, don't make a sound.
A big fat rabbit smiled at me,
'Is it a little boy that I see?'
'Yes, I'm Thomas,' and smiled right back,
'Pleased to meet you, my name's Jack.
Watch if you want, but don't say a word,
be as quiet as a mouse, as still as a bird.'
'Playtime!' roared Jack and blew his whistle,
I jumped with surprise and sat on a thistle!
There were rabbits on bikes, rabbits on scooters,
rabbits in cars tooting their hooters,
sailing in boats, flying in planes,
whizzing around in bright red trains.
Oh what a laugh! Oh what a joy!
'I don't want to be just a boy.
Can I be a rabbit too?'
'Oh no,' said Jack, 'that won't do.
Go to school, learn all you can,
grow big and strong and be a man.'

Jan Hedger

The Mysterious Moon

Silently the moonbeam bridge
Spread itself across the sea.
From the moonscape mountain ridge,
Reached my window, calling me.

In the harbour, ships turned silver.
One unfurled its sails for me.
I walked toward it, lost in wonder,
Climbed aboard and set her free.

Silently I lowered the anchor,
Set the compass, took the helm.
Softly, gently, moved the ship out
Drawn towards the moon's pale realm.

Far below the Earth grows smaller,
As I sail among the stars.
Something glimmers in the distance,
Is it Jupiter or Mars?

On and on along the moonbeam,
What will be at journey's end?
How much time before the morning?
Will I ever sail again?

Patricia Lindsay

Why

Why, asked the child, is water wet?
Why are cornflakes dry?
Why are there holes in a butterfly net?
Do onions make you cry?

Why are tortoises sleepy and slow?
And why are thistles prickly?
Why do glow-worms always glow?
What makes tickles tickly?

Why do feathers float on air?
Why is ice cream cold?
Why does Alice have long hair?
Do rainbows end in a pot of gold?

Where does the sun go when the moon
And stars come out at night?
Why did the dish run away with the spoon?
Why are snowflakes white?

Is the seabed where fish go to sleep?
Which end of a worm's the nose?
Why do chickens say, 'Cheep, cheep'?
And why don't snails have toes?

Why do my peas roll off my fork?
Have potatoes eyes for seeing?
Why does Daddy go to work?
Am I a human being?

Why does an octopus have eight arms?
Are strawberries made of straw?
Do eggs taste better from free-range farms?
Why do people go to war?

Why does a postman wear a hat?
(Perhaps at least you can answer that?)

Norman Bissett

Paper Tiger

It was in the headlines
in all the papers.

A big cat was roaming
the countryside -
a lot of people became so frightened,
a gamekeeper
was asked to lay a trap.

An adventure trip,
like a safari -
the trapper of the big cat,
will be great!

Some people were dressed up
in fancy gear -
a pirate,
policeman and gamekeeper.

Eager to start
after something to eat,
off they went,
quietly into the night -
tip-tip-tip
tap-tap-tap
some spots of rain.

With regret,
all they caught was a pet pig.

Olliver Charles

I Like Bananas!

I like bananas,
They are my favourite food.
I like bananas,
I think they're very good.

My mum says I'm a monkey,
I should live in a tree.
I think it would be funky
If the monkeys lived with me.

I like bananas,
But not when they're still green.
No, green bananas
Are bad monkey cuisine.

Mum says I'll turn yellow,
Same as my favourite fruit.
I'd be a yellow fellow
And I'd wear a yellow suit!

I like bananas,
But not when they turn black.
No black bananas,
Don't make a tasty snack.

Mum doesn't like bananas.
Not yellow, green or black.
When Dad gives Mum bananas,
She gives them to him back.

But I like bananas,
I'd eat them all year long.
I really like bananas,
And they inspired this song!

John Lyons

Mr Nobody

Mr Nobody came to stay
The day that I turned five,
And every grown-up seemed to know
As soon as he'd arrived.

The naughtiest thing he's ever done,
He tried to blame on us,
We've told him if he won't behave,
We'll leave him on the bus.

We know that Mummy sees him,
Cos she has that certain face,
And supposes it just *must* be him,
We smugly rest our case.

He steals (it's always him),
And leaves the lights on in our rooms,
He can't pee straight, he makes us late,
He ate the macaroons.

Sarah Dixon

Fruit Bowl Dance

The orange is doing the tango
The apple is doing the twist
The lemon is doing the polka
All dancing about in the mist.

The lime he performs Pavarotti
Leaping from curtains above
Banana's singing so grotty
When he flies on a pure white dove.

The bowl is used as a bandstand
With the kiwi blowing the horn
And the pineapple sitting beside it
Looking all forlorn.

The disco's on top of the cooker
With the glitter ball sparkling above
The satsuma danced on a felucca
And the apricot's fallen in love.

And then a colossal horn blows
'Attention!' shouts out a prune
'Let's conga,' he said,
'And conga to bed.'
The fruits congaed right under the moon.

Mary Spence

What Is A Gobbie?

(For Rachael)

A Gobbie is a sweetie thing
It's round in a square sort of way
It chews with a bite and a sizzle
And is completely hard thro' and thro' its mizzle

It's quite the done thing
Some say, to eat it on a swing
And it tastes like kisses when you're blue
But be very, very cautious
Cos it's dreadfully sticky, and icky like glue

It's not for sharing - only for you
Not even for your bestest friend
So keep it safe, tied with a bow
Your wonderful, and dear, Gobbie-o!

Kim Taylor

Dragon On Fire

The dragon had his tongue out
To try and cool it down
He sure was on fire
Way down low in his mouth.

He tried his breathing exercises
To blow from way down low
It didn't work - this time around -
His body began to glow.

'Must stop this fire within me,'
He mumbled to himself.
'How am I to do that?'
He queried - as he gazed -

Suddenly it was sorted
For he gave a great big burp!
The fire within shot out
Gone was that dreadful curse.

Cheryl Campbell

Molly's Mop

Molly had a new ten pence piece,
She bought a little mop,
When she started mopping,
She found she couldn't stop.
She mopped the dog,
She mopped the cat,
She even mopped her father's hat.
When her mummy came in
I won't tell you what she said,
But the mop went in the cupboard
And Molly went to bed.

Magdalene Chadwick

Keeping Pets

If boys and girls wish for a pet,
The one thing they must not forget
Is pets require a lot of care,
They look to you to treat them fair,
And you must keep them clean and fed,
If not, then have a toy instead.
You take a toy and have a play
And when you put a toy away
Why, there it stays, both safe and sound
Until next playtime comes around.
But pets must be entitled to
The very best of care from you,
A place where they can have a run,
A place to lie out in the sun,
And if these things you will not do
I'm sure a pet is not for you.

G Andrews

My Park

Bloomed roses and lilies welcome everyone
Butterflies busy sucking sweet nectar

Frogs hopping near the pond which is bright
People busy walking in the warm sunlight

Toddlers smiling at everyone they come across
Some children busy fishing, while some are flying kites

Air is refreshing with scent-filled, gentle wind
Everyone secretly admiring the best park in town

Kumudha Venkatesan

The Story

I laid in my bed, warm and wanted,
Engulfed with love and my bear!
He was special, he never was daunted,
He was mine, never to share.

Brown and silky, with big glass eyes,
Quirky mouth, I just had to kiss,
He'd never tell us any lies,
With him, my life was just bliss.

I loved my mummy, also my dad,
They'd tell me a story at night.
They loved me, even when I was bad,
But I knew when they turned out the light.

Brownie, the bear, was my life,
Whatever you did, he was there.
When I grew up, I'd be his wife,
'Cause I knew forever he'd care.

E Corr

The Old Curiosity Shop

The creaking door opened to the curiosity shop,
What I saw inside gave me quite a shock.
It smelt so musty and damp,
What was that creature sitting under the lamp?
Was it a man or was it a beast?
Sitting there eating a gruesome feast,
Grinding up bones, blood dripping from his chin,
His eyes were shut, so I crept by him.
The shelves were stacked from floor to ceiling,
With things that gave me an eerie feeling,
There were rolls and rolls of big hairy toes
And broken fingernails.
Runny noses and poisonous posies,
Bags of battered fluorescent snails.
Jigsaws with no pieces,
Worms that wore dirty fleeces,
Green shoes without any soles.
Deep-fat fryers that sang like church choirs,
And ugly looking trolls.
Long thin tins that screamed and screamed
Waiting to be set free.
I quickly turned and ran away,
So they couldn't come with me.

Margaret Berry

Children

Never
Call a
Child
A kid
It is not
A child's
Proper name.
You would
Think that
It would
Not matter,
But it
Apparently
Isn't the same.

Nicola Barnes

When You Were Small

My children are all adults now,
Tho' in my heart, still small!
I see them in my mind's eye,
From two, to four feet tall!
As babies, cradled in my arms,
Or toddlers, running, playing,
Listening to stories from a book,
Learning from what I was saying!
I 'see' them playing with their friends,
Laughing in their games,
Discussing what they did at school,
Telling me teachers' names!
Bringing home their homework,
Always above *my* head!
Their academic achievements,
I fear, left me for dead!
I specially loved the holidays,
We went for lots of walks,
No TV in those days,
So lots of time for talks!
The years flew past so quickly,
Now, they've children of their own,
It's a very different world today,
Old values all have flown.
Yet in their children, I see mine!
History is ever repeated,
The action is updated,
But the end result, undefeated!
I am proud of my family,
Four generations to date,
I'm the head of quite a 'dynasty',
Who all, to each other relate!

E M Eagle

Good Manners In Nusopia

When a Nusopian sneezes
And you hear, *'Atishoo!'*
It is of course polite
To respond with, 'Bless you.'
However, in Nusopia
When someone says, 'Bless you',
Saying 'Handangaranga'
Is the right thing to do.
As soon as 'Handangaranga' is said
You should shout, 'Yung! Dung! Hung!'
With one hand on your head.
At this point, one should hum,
Holding a rose;
If you don't have this flower
You should instead hold your nose.
It's then polite to sing
With a mouth full of eggs,
Smiling upside down
Looking back through your legs.
It's not necessary,
But considered good luck,
To let one egg drop down,
While you quack like a duck.
Now, Nusopians strive to be
Polite, civil and pleasing,
But most of all, they generally
Try to avoid sneezing.

Joe Campbell

The Magical Koala
(Who Said Teddies Never Do Anything?)

Every night and every day
I sit here waiting for you
You need me and I need you
If you're in pain, let's make this clear
I am magical and can make it disappear
When you're down, I'll make you smile
And if you smile, share it I will
Everywhere you are, I am there
Everywhere you've been, I've been too
As old as you I am, as old as me are you
Together forever we will be
Watching over you
Like you watch over me
I am the magical koala
And you can't get rid of me!

David Maguire

Our Farm

We live in the country,
In fact on a farm,
Look after our animals,
They don't come to harm.

My dad milks the cows
Inside our big shed,
They make lovely milk,
Good for you, it's said.

I feed the pink pigs
Who grunt as they eat,
Sometimes they are greedy,
Always have dirty feet!

My mother makes cheese
In a very large bowl,
She stirs it around,
Tastes good, on the whole!

My sister feeds hens,
Who peck at their grain,
Lay eggs in their house,
They don't like the rain!

Our dogs mind the sheep,
With help from our dad,
They bring them from fields
When the weather is bad.

We all have jobs
Round our lovely farmhouse,
When our animals sleep,
They're as quiet as a mouse!

Maureen Westwood O'Hara

Just Me

I wish I were my teddy
I wouldn't have to wash
And clean my teeth or comb my hair,
And all that grown-up bosh.

I wouldn't have to go to school,
I'd stay at home all day.
But if I were my teddy,
I wouldn't be there to play.

I wish I were my teddy,
Now I'll confide in you,
While I would be my teddy,
I'd be my own self too.

Gilbert Burns

Don't Like Dolls

Of all my toys I love the best
My favourite's teddies, plain, undressed
I can't stand dollies - stupid things
Not even ones that Santa brings
I wish he'd kept his rotten dolls
And given me MGs, Fords or Rolls
I'd rather have a humming top,
A vacuum cleaner, broom or mop
I'd love another teddy - true
But really - I've got one or two
Perhaps I'll be content with those
And dress them in my brother's clothes
I hope I have convinced you now
I don't find dolls much of a wow
I love my teds to cuddle around
When I'm in bed, all snuggled down
I'll say again and yet again
Don't like dolls!

R W Meacheam

Sidney Becomes A Seagull

I was playing on the beach making castles with my friend,
I said, 'I'd like to be a seagull - just for one weekend.'
He said, 'My dad's a wizard, he can sort it if you want.
You have to tell your mum and dad, they'll wonder
where you've gone.'

My mum was busy knitting and didn't want to be disturbed.
'Sidney - just do what you want . . .' So I became a bird.
I stole Bully Barker's pasty, then terrified his mother.
I laughed as Bully screamed with fear when I
dive-bombed his brother.

Then there was Gertie Gossip, who lived along our street.
I swooped low, and let it go . . . all over her sheets.
I was feeling rather peckish and waddled home for tea,
My mother was still knitting and didn't notice me.

I swallowed my jam sandwich and before I went to bed,
I said goodnight to my mother and pecked her on the head.
Next day the fun was over - just after half-past three,
I was screeching down a chimney when I turned back into me.

Someone called my mother, 'Your Sidney's on the roof!'
She said, 'I'm busy knitting - there's nothing I can do.'
So the fireman brought his ladder and the town came out to stare,
But no one ever really knew just how I'd got up there.

Paula Hill

Cleaning My Room

My mum is cleaning my room.
She's tidying up my books and my bed.
She's trying to find the carpet,
Her face is going red.

My mum is cleaning my room.
She's huffing and puffing a lot.
Why is it she's allowed to swear
But I'm definitely not?

My mum is cleaning my room.
She's moaning that it's not fair.
I'm watching her and laughing
'Cause there's dust all in her hair.

My mum is cleaning my room.
She's getting really stressed.
If I didn't know her
I would definitely think she's possessed.

Hold on, what's going on?
My mum was cleaning my room
But now she's shouting at me
And handing me the broom.

I am cleaning my room.
It's taking me all day and night.
My mum is laughing at me now
Surely that can't be right!

Rachel Hobson

The Night Before

The night before, the nerves are high,
Don't have a clue how I'm going to get by.
Facts and figures swimming round in my head,
Can't get to sleep, I'm just lying in bed.
Competitive tendering, what was its aim?
And the person who thought of it, what was his name?
Trig formulae still in my mind, in the way,
Don't need them now, I failed maths yesterday!

Rebecca Muir (16)

A Secret!

A secret is a secret as long as nobody else knows,
But a secret would not be a secret if not one person knew,
A burning desire to tell could ruin everything,
And to ruin everything would be to tell as a burning desire,
A secret comes from your heart, which is magical,
And something magical is the heart where secrets are kept,
A secret is a feeling, which is not to be denied,
And to deny a secret would be denying a feeling,
Listen to your heart where feelings are true
And a feeling is a secret, so keep this one to you.

Darrion Warwick-Hart (14)

Monster, Monster!

The sun is down. It's night-time now.
I can't even hear the moo of a cow.
The monsters roam,
They let out a mighty groan.
I have to stay hidden,
These creatures are forbidden.
If one finds me,
I'm a goner you see.
Oh no! One's caught my eye.
He thinks I'm a spy.
Hide, hide!
His jaw is really wide,
I look like an ant to him,
And one that's really slim.
I duck and I roll,
I go down a hole.
I did that and I don't know how,
But at least I'm safe . . . for now!

Sam Delaney (10)

Daylight And Moonlight

Daylight comes and daylight goes
Every day I see the sun, then every night I see the moon
And it is so bright that I want to feel it
And it is so lovely that I want to feel it again and again
The sun is lovely and yellow
The sun's rays are bright and shiny
The moon comes in and goes out and fills our lives with magic
The moon comes in different shapes and sizes
Which one do you think is the best?

Shayo Oshinbolu (8)

Gutted

Watching Swindon play Brighton, my heart is racing
It looks like we're winning, this is so amazing
With seconds to go, Brighton score
I feel gutted, I can say no more
Penalty kicks, we go first
I feel as if I am going to burst
Our first ball is in, Brighton's is too
Come one Mooney, you know what to do
Oh no, Mooney, what are you doing?
Was it because the crowd was booing?

The match is over, my team has lost
Hold back the tears, I can only just
I thought we were through
I thought it for certain
I said to my mum as she closed the curtain.
'Never mind, they did their best my dear.'
I know she was right, well there is always next year.

It's the morning after the night before
There's one thing I know for sure
I am still your biggest ever fan
There's just one thing I really want if I can
Because money is tight, you know what it's like
I so want to be a season ticket holder
With all of your fans to stand shoulder to shoulder
To shout, 'Come on you reds!' at the top of my voice
To see all of my fabulous Swindon Town boys
Next season there is one thing I know for certain
I will be shouting, 'We did it!' as my mum closes the curtain.

Matthew Higgins (11)

Paradise Island

Palm trees swaying in the breezy wind,
Golden sand, warm and wet,
Coconuts falling from the trees, blowing in the breeze.
The sea is nice and calm,
The sun is golden and warm,
Ice creams melting with the heat,
People sunbathing on the golden sand,
Cool cans keep filling up the bag.
People playing and swimming in the sea,
People squirting each other with water pistols.
Suncream being slapped on the children,
Nice blue skies, not a cloud in sight.
I'm lying down on the golden sand and
Keep going scuba-diving to see all the fish.

Gary Muchmore (13)

A Tower

(This is the one poem I wrote during my childhood, at the age of 10)

I am a tower,
With strength and power.
I can hold one hundred people,
And I am higher than any steeple.
A flag sticks out of my head,
White with a cross, which is red.
Rain doesn't bother me,
I have a nice shower.
It is such a nice life
To be a tower.

Margaret A Greenhalgh

I'm Learning

I'm apprenticed to a wizard,
The finest in the land,
If I mix his herbs and potions,
He'll teach me to use a wand.

I've conjured up a unicorn,
But he hasn't got a tail,
Then I practised on the cat,
Who turned into a snail.

My master's hair turned purple,
His left foot is a hoof,
I must reverse this magic
Or he'll surely hit the roof.

I tried to spell it backwards,
Then I tried it upside down,
But all I ended up doing
Was changing him into a clown.

I'm really just a learner,
Too young and not too bright,
Now my wand is in the cupboard,
Until I can get it right.

Doris Green

Dog Talk

I'm wet and cold and dirty
And my mistress won't be pleased
When I drip across the carpet
Leaving muddy footprints there.

It really wasn't my fault
That I fell into the pond,
I had to chase that naughty cat
That tries to catch the birds.

So I ran as fast as possible
Across the lawn and jumped -
But I didn't jump quite far enough
And I landed in the pond.

That cat sat in the oak tree
And I'm sure it laughed at me
And the fish were most indignant
At my sudden mighty splash.

Now I've been told that I must look
Before I chase the cat
And either take a longer jump
Or bypass watery spots.

But as I doze before the fire
How nice and warm and dry
I dream that cat falls in the pond -
'Three cheers!' is what I cry.

Roma Davies

An English Springtime

The purple carpet unfurls to welcome Spring
Trees are festooned with blossom
Bouncing squirrels eagerly wave their bushy flag-tails
All is ready

Spring majestically waltzes into the woods
Dancing around the crocus and each cheerful daffodil
The snow bows down as Spring passes by
Melting into the awakening earth

Blackbirds and wrens alight upon a leaf, trilling a merry fanfare.
'Ah,' chuckles Spring, taking a deep breath of crisp morning air,
'Ah, this is England.'

Robin in his royal redbreast nods.
Spring, the elusive globetrotter had come home.

Ruth M Ellett

The Snail

The snail likes the rain as it slides along the pane,
It shivers and shakes as it meets its mates.
The snail likes the rain.

The snail leaves a trail as it slides across the floor.
The snail leaves a trail as it climbs upon my door.

The snail had a race but it was too slow to keep the pace.
The snail moved a mile as it fell onto a pile.

The snail got stuck as it slid across a rock.
The snail looked funny as it slid into a sock.

The snail looked pale as it slid across the floor.
So please go away little snail, and don't climb upon my door.

Marina Smith

Harry Who?

His real name was Harry-Ho
Who lived a little time ago,
When people provided home-made fun
In the land of EE-bah-gum.

A popular man about the town,
A local version of the circus clown.
But his acts were put on in the streets
Where people watching had no seats.

The audience would stand around and clap
This very talented kind of chap.
Without a stage, the gas-lit scene was there
On stone laid flags in the open air.

With longish hair and a longish face,
Harry would soon set up the pace
In a form of dance you may not know,
Of heel-and-heel and toe-and-toe.

The noise of his clatter would arouse the dogs,
For Harry's footwear was a pair of clogs.
Clippety-clop, clippety-clip, crash, bang, clatter,
The tempo grew in speed like it did not matter.

In-between these rhythmical turns of zest,
Harry would sometimes remove his vest
And make little acrobatic twists and twirls,
Astonishing all the watching boys and girls.

To give their backing to this lively little man,
People threw coins into an empty beans can,
And he would come again, you know,
Giving great pleasure with heel and toe.

Regis

My Friend

      My friend likes bees because they sting.
They fly and land on anything.
They look fluffy, cute and bubbly,
      But are mean and hurt when they're angry.

      I don't like bumblebees, they're boring.
      They sting you in summer if you're snoring.
They eat flowers, yuck.
But seem happy as a pig in muck.

      My friend likes bees because they sting.
      When you're stung, you can't stop itching.
He likes to itch and squirm about,
      Like Incy-Wincey Spider climbing up the waterspout.

Paula Kelly

Head Lice Are Not Very Nice!

When at school with all your friends
You can share your books and pens
But never share a brush or hat
For head lice will discover that
They can travel really easy
Unless your hair is nice and greasy!
They like it when your hair is down
So tie it up and twirl it round
If you swap a band or slide
You give the lice a chance to hide
On your head unless you comb
Makes the perfect head lice home!
They cannot jump or sing a song
But even if your hair's not long
Those naughty lice will move their eggs
Your strands of hair become their beds
Your head may feel really itchy
This could make you very twitchy
So please make sure you're combing right
So it's only you asleep at night!

Anne-Marie Howard

Thoughts In My Head

It all starts when I go to bed,
All these thoughts go through my head.
Is there someone else in the room with me?
I'm too scared to open my eyes and see.
I hear a noise, are they under my bed?
I wish these thoughts would go from my head.
I get up the courage to open my eyes,
Shock, horror and a nasty surprise.
There is somebody standing by the door,
They definitely weren't there before.
They are very big and so tall too,
There's only one thing for me to do.
I shout and scream for my dad,
he's there in a shot, I'm so glad.
'What is the matter? Why did you shout?'
'Somebody's by the door, throw them out.'
He puts on the light for me to see,
There's nobody there, I have to agree.
It's just my nice pink dressing gown
On the back of the door, hanging down.
The light is out, he's checked under the bed,
Oh I wish these thoughts would stay out of my head.

Teresa Smith

Sir Geoffrey Rides

Here's a story of Sir Geoffrey the Bold,
Who chased hidden treasures, this tale to be told.
He sought the purple dragon and to find a queen,
And began an adventure, for us to scream.

Sir Geoffrey wore his armour and of course,
Found his old sword and yelled for his horse.
From his beloved castle, through the forest he rode,
Till a green warty witch turned him into a toad.
So a toad rode a horse, till a silver fairy set him free,
He bowed most kindly, then crashed into a tree.

Sir Geoffrey awoke in a freezing cold mountain,
Chained to a rock, below a black fountain.
'How did I get here?' 'You're my dinner you fool.'
Sir Geoffrey wasn't hungry as he spotted the ghoul.
A crack to the head from a lady fair, spared him from its supper,
A ghoul unfed and off he sped, that greedy old 'Gruppa'.

Before Sir Geoffrey could speak, the purple dragon uncoiled,
To keep the story going and knights to be boiled.
She gave him a taste of her hot dragon breath,
Yellow, green and red, scared Sir Geoffrey to death.
So he baked very quickly in his glowing armour.
But he'd sworn not to hurt her, only to capture, not harm her.
For soon he was cooled down by a bucket of water,
'Rescue me, my lord, I'm King Tingle's daughter!'

So they both agreed, the purple dragon was truly a charmer,
Who was sorry to them all, and cross with the ghoul
And owed Sir Geoffrey new armour.
So she flew them all home from the mountains and clouds,
To their fairytale wedding, that lit up the crowds,
And wise purple dragon, she left them her treasure,
As wedding gifts and happy endings, plus a story for good measure.

Philip Lowe

Playing At Recycling

Ruth made a large house from cardboard
It was as big as the ironing board
Ruth played in it all day
But Mum threw it away
So Ruth said to Mum, 'Now I'm bored.'

Then Ruth made a big submarine
Out of cartons from old Mr Sheen
She got in a mess
She spilt glue on her dress
And got stuck to the blinking machine.

Her sister washed Ruth down with a hose
Ruth gave her a punch on the nose.
'I was trying to help,'
Sister said with a yelp
As Ruth stomped upstairs in wet clothes.

Liz Brown

School

School
The place of so-called learning
Yeah, right
My books learn more than I do
Things I hate about school
Dinner queues
Student loos
English after maths
Crummy packed lunches
I hate pasties

School
The place of so-called fun
Break time, break time
It's more like hate time
All you do is carry your bag around
And think of strict teachers
Football
One fun thing
I wouldn't go to school
If there was no football
Kick, kick, kick
Score.

Jack Maiden (11)

Me

(Written for Tilly Mae aged 17 months)

Meet my feet, they're for standing
When I jump, they're for landing

Meet my hands, they're for touch
Grabbing, tickling, learning much

Meet my eyes, they're for seeing
Toys, smiles and mirrors with me in

Meet my mouth, it's for food
Well anything, if it looks good

Meet my ears, they're for hearing
Singing, laughing, shouting and cheering

Meet my nose, it's for smell
If there is food I can tell

So here I am, all of me
Toes that wiggle, to eyes that see

Emma Bulley

I Thought I Saw A Fairy

I thought I saw a fairy,
Her friends looked kind of scary,
I think one was a goblin,
He looked like he was hobbling.
Hmm, maybe that's why they're called hobgoblins,
Because they walk with a limp,
Or was that a little imp?

I don't know, but they all looked kind of scary,
I much preferred the fairy!
She had a pretty pink dress and a crown,
But on her face she wore a frown,
Because her hair was all a mess,
And there was mud on her pretty pink dress.

She said, 'A monster did it.
Big and hairy, really quite scary.'

That reminded me of another,
Not quite a monster, but my brother.

He has big feet and smells,
He gets quite angry and yells.
He broke all my pretty shells.

They were sat on their shelf looking around,
When he came up the stairs banging around,
They all fell off and smashed on the ground.

I asked why he was covered in muck,
He said he got caught up in a ruck,
He slipped on the mud,
And then with a thud,
He landed in a big wet puddle,
Got himself in a right old muddle.

Big brothers are meant to be clever,
But not my big brother, Trevor.
I reckon the fairy was getting revenge,
On my big smelly brother, Trevor,
I'll think kindly of her forever.

Kim Davies

Butterflies

Mummy! Come quick
Look what I've found
It's a colourful butterfly
There, on the ground
Of beautiful colours
Some orange and spotty
Others plain white
Some colourful and dotty
I'm going to sit down
They move more when I stand
Maybe I can get closer
Sshh! There's one on my hand
I wonder where my butterflies go
When the weather is colder
And the skies
Fill with snow?
I'll miss all the butterflies
When Christmas songs we sing
But it's just a few months
They'll be back in the spring
Lovely butterflies
In my garden today
If I was a butterfly
I'd fly away
Butterflies, butterflies
Fly high as a tower
I'll see you next spring
Caressed in flower.

Dan McPheat

Bluebell Wood

The elves and the fairies live deep down in the wood
In little leaf houses held together with mud
Big people can't see them, but little children can
And today they're having a party, that's the plan.

Josh, Ollie and Ethan are invited to play
With all their little friends on this special day
And Bandit, the dog, he will be coming as well
Down to the bluebell wood's very own fairy dell.

Pickwick and Timber are the two oldest elves
And they are using the oak tree branches as shelves
To put Tipsey and Whisper's tiny fairy cakes
Just before the sun fills the sky as the dawn breaks.

Pumkin and Tuck are making dandelion wine
Which they will all drink later in the sunshine
Fidgety Frog is splashing around in the stream
Watching the elves and the fairies work as a team.

Then the three little boys arrive, each on his bike
Because that is what all of them do really like
Bandit watches them cycle up hilly places
And wags his tail when he sees their happy faces.

Bumble and Bliss fly over to join in the fun
Their gossamer wings shimmering in the sun
A magical scene witnessed by a faithful dog
And a small green inquisitive fidgety frog.

Ann Blair

Cheeky Frog

(For Wallis)

A frog hopped on my lap today and then up on my shoulder.
He turned and whispered in my ear, 'Could I be a little bolder?
If you kiss my cheek, I'll croak and change into a prince.
I'm tall, dark and handsome and you can call me Vince.'
As he asked, I kissed his cheek and there before my eyes
He transformed into this handsome man, but only half my size.
'OK, I lied!' he cried aloud. 'I'm not as tall as you thought.'
'And I see your hair is not your own, in fact it has been bought.
At least you have a gorgeous face, you've achieved one out of three.'
Vince stood there, fluttered his lashes and smiled at me with glee.
Unfortunately he coughed a bit and out flew his false teeth.
I can't believe a little frog could lie beyond belief.
'Although you have a pretty face, everything else you are lacking,
I think I'll do the kindest thing, kiss you again and send you packing.'
As I kissed his cheek once more, in front of me he shrunk,
Hopped away with a hiccup and a wink, and I realised he was drunk.
So if, by chance, you see a frog that asks you for a smooch
Say, 'Go away! You ugly toad. I'd rather kiss a pooch.'

Juju

Noisy Hullabaloo

What a noisy place is Hullabaloo,
Where car horns honk the whole day through,
You can hear it for miles around.
Where the tin can factory bangs all day,
And folks can't hear what you have to say,
For pneumatic drills make a fine to do
In that noisy place called Hullabaloo.
The animals are mixed up too.
The cows go 'Baa' and the sheep go 'Moo',
The cats all bark and the dogs go 'Mew',
In that noisy place called Hullabaloo.
The birds all croak and the frogs all sing,
And you can't hear a word when the telephones ring,
In noisy Hullabaloo.
If you think it's quiet when they're asleep,
And in Hullabaloo you won't hear a peep,
Well you're wrong, they all snore
And the owls go, 'Whoooo',
In dreadfully noisy Hullabaloo.

Margaret B Baguley

The Ringarangaroo

Professor Shocks, he opened a box, and out popped a ringarangaroo,
He took it to his study, because he didn't know what to do.
Now a ringarangaroo is an insect from Planet X to you,
They say it's ten billion miles from Earth, I wonder if it's true?
He gave it a drink of orange juice, and a piece of jam and bread,
Suddenly it jumped up an said, 'I like that, I'll have a little bit more.'
It didn't look where it was, and banged against the door.
'I'd like to taste some proper food, because we live on microbes there,
I'm enjoying this fine weather, because ours is never fair.
Would you take a photograph of me, so show my ma and pa?
If you should come to our planet, you'll not find such things as a car.
Have you got a bed for me, to relax in instead of this box?
I was very lucky coming here, I could have been crushed by rocks.
I really fancy living here, that's what I'd like to do.
Do you think you could invite us all to live here in this place?'
'How many of you are there?' he said with a grin on his face.
'Oh, only about nine hundred billion, and that's not counting the wives.
Of course if we could settle here, we'd all lead different lives,
You wouldn't have to worry, we would live on jam and bread.
If you agree, Professor, that's all that needs to be said.
Just take me to Cape Canaveral, and blast me back into space,
We'll be back before you know it, we'll take over this
                                        magnificent place.'

James Ayrey

Garden

I played in the garden all day today,
In and out, talking to Mum. She said
Something about making her spill all her flour,
So I went and picked her some.
She didn't seem pleased by my handful of blooms,
Though I thought I was being good.
She tried to explain, but she shouted a lot
And I never understood.

I offered to clean the mud off the floor,
And ran out to fetch the trowel.
But when I went in, she screamed out, *'Boo-oots!'*,
And chased me away with the towel.
Y'know, my mum can shout really loud.
No wonder her head's so sore.
I could hear her right from the back of our garden,
And so could the lady next door, and next door.

If only I'd not dropped her watch in the bath . . .
Still, she loves me anyway.
I could tell, by her smile as she put me to bed.
. . . And tomorrow's another day.

Bill Eden

Ma's Tabby

By the pillow
like a silent show
sits Ma's tabby
fat and flabby
with fur like silk
white as pure milk
watching me eat
as I quietly sit
at the table
quite, quite unable
to move away
for then, anyway,
he wants the fish
on my poor dish
and I can't tell
I wish him well:
I'm hungry too
but he's muscle 'n' sinew
and in a fight
he's always right.

Sumanta Sanyal

This Evening

This evening I intend to
Play with my Nintendo,
My PlayStation too.
(ie, My PlayStation 2!)
Along with my Xbox,
Borrowed by my dad from his ex-boss!

Andy Field

Dreams

Dreams are full of wonder,
Dreams are full of happiness,
Dreams are for you and me
To share with everyone.
Dreams are made out of your imagination
Which is full of beautiful sights.
And maybe they might come true one day,
If you keep on dreaming too.

Emily Lewis (10)

Kylie's Hamster

I opened Kylie's door and what did I see,
But two little brown eyes staring up at me.
Ah! Poor little angel in his cage all scruffy,
But he looks so cute, small, brown and fluffy.
As I walked to his cage, he quickly ran to the door,
He knows he is coming out to play some more.

In his see-through ball he whizzes round the room,
I'll clean his cage and put him back in soon.
I'll put in fresh water, chocolate treats, and bedding,
And all around his cage he will be treading.
He will get all excited and have plenty to eat,
Then curl up in a ball and go to sleep.

Dorothy Slevin

Hey Mister Clown

A lonely little clown with a painted smile
Sits in the corner of a circus tent
And his eyes are filled with tears
Cos he can't make the children laugh anymore
The jokes that he tells aren't funny now
Cos he's done them all for years

Then in walks a boy with a smile on his face
And says, 'Hey Mister Clown, you were great.
I came here because I was feeling down
And now you've put a smile on my face!'

So said Mister Clown to the little boy,
'I thought everyone was fed up with me
And I should just walk out the door.'
But the little boy said, 'Don't you worry now,
You made me laugh more than the others did,
Much more than the clowns I saw before!

They say that the oldest jokes are the best
And that's one thing that I do believe.'
Then the little boy turned and he left the clown thinking,
I still make 'em laugh it may seem!

Melinda Penman

Two Troublesome Pups

Two little dogs in their kennels one day,
One said to the other, 'Let's go out to play.'
So one played with his ball
And the other chased a cat,
But the cat jumped the fence,
So that was that.
Now both little dogs just didn't know what to do,
They were both wishing that they had a bone to chew,
So off they went to dig up the ground,
But unluckily for them, there were no bones to be found.
They dug and they dug and there was dirt everywhere,
But both little dogs just hadn't a care.
Later their owner came outside to them
To see what they were doing,
'Oh no, I don't believe it,
It's the garden hose they're chewing!
Stop that you two,' she shouted,
Then both dogs looked so sad,
They loved their owner very much,
But didn't like it when she was mad.
She took them both inside,
Then gave them a bath,
Then she smiled and started to laugh.
They licked her hands and licked her face,
These little dogs were no longer in disgrace.

Margaret Holyman

The Magical Tree

The fairies were dancing, one starry night
When the moon was out, shining bright
Playing with their friend, little Polly Pixie
Around the large, magical tree

The disobedient gnome, who lived with the goblins
Left his home, and appeared in fairyland with a grin
He sat himself down, near the wandering river
The dusks were awoken, with the noise by this figure

They made such a squeal, the pixie flew near
The gnome being naughty pinched her ear
She screamed, till the fairy Godmother appeared
She waved her wand three times, the gnome disappeared

He landed on the tree, the tree was really annoyed
To find this creature there, who whimpered and cried
The tree wavered to the leaves, that threw him so high
The gnome nearly went to the moon, way up in the vast sky

The Fairy Godmother waved her wand again, the gnome landed
with a thump
By then his nose was red and raw, and so swollen, with a lump
The Fairy Godmother felt sorry, and waved her wand thrice
Just wondering if he would be taught a lesson, and really think twice

Well, he went back to the goblins, his home so far away
But will he forget what happened, through his mischievous way?
Will he ever go back to Fairyland? Well, it may take some time
Where the magical tree still stands, and the leaves sway to a rhyme.

Especially when the gentle breeze blows, to the warmth of the spring
Children, do not go to Fairyland so far away, where the fairies dance
in a ring
But, you may see a pixie in the garden, or the meadows
But it is too late in the deep of the night, where the river flows.

Jean P McGovern

Bizarre Beasts

Although ant armies attack and
Buzzing bugs bite
Contented cud-chewing cows
Discover delicate daydreams

Elderly elephants encountering
Fascinating flamingos
Graceful gazelles greeting
Happy hippos

Imagine impatient ibis
Joining jaunty joyful jays
Khaki kangaroos keeping
Lonely llamas laughing

Mischievous monkeys making
Nervous newts neurotic
Orange orang-utans outraging
Precious posing parakeets

Querulous quail quickly
Rejecting radiant robins
Spurning sulking sparrows

Terrible tarantulas taunting
Unhappy unicorns
Vibrant vipers vanishing
While wary wombats wait

Xenophobic
Yellow yetis yawn yet
Zany zebras zing.

Patricia Smith

The Grumpy Fairy

I woke up this morning feeling quite grumpy,
My wand was all bent and my flying was bumpy.
Feeling so cross I got up to no good,
I didn't do things that a good fairy should.

I went to a school and hid teacher's pen,
And then when she found it - *I hid it again!*
Tipped over some drinks at two children's parties,
Then jumped on the cakes and pinched all the Smarties!

The tooth fairy told my mum what I'd done,
So that was the end of *my* naughty fun.
If I came to your house, please forgive my mad ways
But even *good* fairies, can have *bad days!*

Susan Lorkins

World's Greatest Need

Of what we have less of and need more of are:
children with dreams, and willpower,
children who cannot choose shortcuts
as an honest means of achieving success.
Who know that illness yielded destroys
lasting integrity of mankind,
who know the value of education
and the joy of its celebration.
Children who understand seasons
and expect challenges of each season,
who are just and true to their peers,
even when their parents are preaching individualism.
Honest children in schools who cannot tell believable lies,
even when they are policed by fears.
Children who know the wealth of character
and its compelling favours.
Children who are prepared to be professionals
in their chosen careers and on time.

Anyatonwu Ikechukwu Collins

If I Were Mrs Santa Claus

If I were Mrs Santa Claus
I'd make a wish for you,
touch every star up in the sky
to make your dreams come true.

I'd fill your stockings full of love
and laughter for all years,
I'd be the blanket on your bed
to dry away your tears.

I'd be the light within the dark
to shine through all the nights
and hold your hands and keep them warm
and safe from any fright.

I'd be your smile for happy times
to keep within your heart,
to greet each day with bright new thoughts
and laughter from the start.

Would you be a super hero
or a princess fair and true?
The future of your fondest dreams
would be brought from me to you.

And all the beauty in the world
would ride on angels' wings
and light upon your window sill
for Christmas Day to bring.

Now you be good and say your prayers
and Christmas Day you'll find,
that Mrs Santa Claus is real
in each kind heart and mind.

Patricia Jenkins Hieke-Fish

Sweet Dreams

Go to sleep now little one
Find your dreams once more
As now it's time to close your eyes
And dream your dreams away

Don't be scared now little one
I'm here to keep you safe
Because if you wake so suddenly
I'm here right by your side

It's dark outside
And night is here
Be calm, now close your eyes
Dreams are waiting for you
Search them, you will see

I'll see you in the morning
You can tell me all you saw
Go to sleep now little one
Sweet dreams
Sweet dreams once more.

Louise Wigmore

Observation

I'm a crack in the pavement,
I sit here all the time,
I'm the source of enjoyment
As children dodge the line.

I'm a crack in the pavement,
I sit here far from grace.
I'm the sidewalk gazement
As people step on my face.

I'm a crack in the pavement,
I can hear the dreaded drill,
I feel a sudden movement
As around me the workmen fill.

I was a crack in the pavement,
I've been levered from my rest,
I'm about to become a remnant
As the hammer hits my chest.

A Chaldecott

There Came A Wave . . .

There came a wave like a great hand,
Grabbing everything on the land,
Its fingers of foam, circling round,
Uprooting trees, raising homes to the ground,
It aimed its fist at everything in sight,
Nothing could survive this dreadful might,
People ran in and out in time with the tide,
Nowhere to go and nowhere to hide,
The hand was born in the belly of the ocean,
Fed by plates creating the potion,
It grew in fury, it grew in power,
The anger to be unleashed within the hour,
No one knew what was on the way,
People were working, children at play,
A shriek of surprise as somebody saw,
A huge wall of white horses galloping ashore,
The beasts dissolved under the heat,
Sweeping hundreds of thousands off their feet,
There was crashing and crunching and tearing apart,
Seeping its way into everyone's heart,
Lives were lost, bodies found,
Brutally killed by a hungry hound,
When the punch came with the force of an army,
The few that survived understood the meaning of 'tsunami'.

Lily May Usher (12)

Anchor Books Information

We hope you have enjoyed reading this book - and that you will continue to enjoy it in the coming years.

If you like reading and writing poetry drop us a line, or give us a call, and we'll send you a free information pack.

Alternatively if you would like to order further copies of this book or any of our other titles, then please give us a call or log onto our website at www.forwardpress.co.uk

**Anchor Books Information
Remus House
Coltsfoot Drive
Peterborough
PE2 9JX**

(01733) 898102